RULES

FOR

BILLIARDS AND POOL

And an Illustrated Catalogue of

BRIGGS' BILLIARD TABLES

AND

Billiard Furnishings.

PUBLISHED BY

OLIVER L. BRIGGS

970 Washington Street

BOSTON, U. S. A.

This book is published for the use of all interested in Billiards. The information has been very carefully collected, the rules carefully revised. and no pains spared to make it of real value.

"The best cushion in the market!"

WILLIAM P. MARSHALL, Boston Globe.

We take this opportunity to thank the public for the hearty support they have given us in putting forward a billiard cushion of real merit. Now, that it has become popular in New England, we can only say that the present high standard of the ELECTRIC CUSHIONS will always be maintained.

OLIVER L. BRIGGS,
FREDERICK H. BRIGGS.

FROM THE PARKER HOUSE, BOSTON.

DEAR SIR :

We have tested and used your recent invention, the new ELECTRIC CUSHION now in use at the Parker House, Boston, and consider it far superior to any cushion we have played on.

Signed by the best players at the Parker House.

Popularity Follows the ELECTRIC CUSHIONS.

HIGHEST AWARDS.

The Briggs tables have never been beaten.

The Briggs billiard tables have the unrivaled record of never being beaten in any competitive exhibition, although they have entered into competition with all the principal concerns that have ever done business in New England.

The number of diplomas taken are too numerous to mention here. The first medal received was awarded in 1876, then followed the exhibition of 1878, with five billiard exhibits, including the best known manufacturers in the country. The ONLY medal awarded was given to the Briggs table.

The Mechanics Fair of 1881 added another, the highst given that year.

The year 1884 added two more medals—gold and silver—a bronze this year being awarded to another maker.

The 1890 medal of silver (no gold that year), was awarded for superior workmanship and finish, thus marking an era of better construction than had hitherto been deemed necessary.

The medal of 1892 was awarded by the Mechanics' Fair to the ELECTRIC CUSHIONS for being the greatest advancement ever made in billiard cushions.

A new Billiard Light, the ELECTRIC CUSHIONS.

THE BILLIARD ROOM.

In a private residence or a public place the billiard room should be first of all, convenient.

The game of billiards affords the best recreation known, in that it combines moderate, healthful, physical and mental exercise. Already many business and professional men and women are recognizing this, and are seeking comfortable home-like surroundings to pass their hour or two with the cue; therefore make your billiard-room light, comfortable, airy, easy of access, and keep your tables in good repair.

SPACE REQUIRED FOR BILLIARD TABLE.

Space required for 5 x10 Table . . . . 15 x20 feet.
Space required for 4½x 9 Table . . . . 14½x19 feet.
Space required for 4 x 8 Table . . . . 13 x17 feet.

The above spaces may be varied by shortening cues.

(5)

Billiards in 1860.

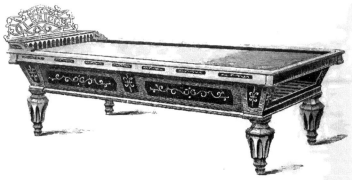

SIPPIO TABLE.

How to Tip Cues.

First—Give the end of the cue a square, clean, smooth surface, slightly depressed in the centre. A cue cutter will be found useful in doing this.

Second—Select your tip a trifle larger than the cue, if a high tip is preferred, pound with a hammer until the " spread " is taken out. Rub the bottom with sand-paper a few times.

Third—Apply a small amount of glue to the end of the cue, and place the tip in position, holding it there by a cue press, or some weighty substance.

Fourth—When dry, cut with a sharp knife the protruding leather, and finish with first coarse, then fine sand paper, shaping the tip as desired.

Purchased Opinions not needed for ELECTRIC CUSHIONS

LATEST PATENT, 1892.

◁ THE **ELECTRIC** CUSHION

TRADE MARK.

Highest award, Mechanics' Fair, 1892.

From a billiard cushion, players demand absolute accuracy, "English" taking power, quickness, and durability, including in this term, action unchanged by atmospheric or other causes. The ELECTRIC are the only cushions that have satisfactorily united all these points. A very ingenious combination of rubber, wire and air produces the long-thought impossible union of great speed and "English" taking power, while none of the other important features are sacrificed.

The results from the introduction, a year ago, of these cushions are surprising. With a business more than doubled, with numberless unsolicited testimonials, we feel warranted in saying the ELECTRIC CUSHION is without a peer.

The ELECTRIC CUSHIONS are quick.
They will please yourself, your friends, and your customers.
They will wear well.
They have all the advantages of wire, rubber and air cushions.
They have nothing but the best of material used in their construction.
They will just suit 99 out of 100 billiard players.

SLOW CUSHIONS.

Recognizing the fact that a few accustomed to the older, slow cushions, used in certain parts of the country, have not yet regulated their game to the modern ELECTRIC CUSHIONS, we have made arrangements to furnish a slow cushion to any that may desire it, but will do so only when especially ordered.

PRICES.

ELECTRIC CUSHIONS	$50.00
SLOW CUSHION	35.00

The ELECTRIC CUSHIONS have no Rival.

The Briggs Tables.

The more exacting demands of the present time have encouraged us to build extra well made, well finished tables that will withstand severe climatic changes without becoming weak and shaky in the joints. To the expense of keeping the older, cheaper made tables in repair, is due the popularity of billiards in clubs, where all such expenditures are divided among many.

A table made as ours are now, and fitted with the ELECTRIC CUSHIONS, will be found always ready for use, and need but a trifling amount spent for repairs, as many unsolicited testimonials from well-known men will show.

Popular Styles.

STYLE 26. Is made of solid quartered oak or mahogany, finished light or antique to suit taste. This is a table that for general use can be highly recommended.

STYLE 27. This style is sold for residences chiefly, and is of solid quartered white oak or San Domingo mahogany. An effective and elegant table.

STYLE 28. Is made of oak. This is a very neat table, easily kept clean, attractive to the eye and popular.

STYLE 27

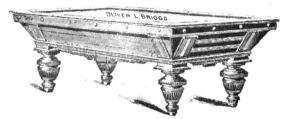

STYLE 26.

STYLE 28

Billiard Room Fittings.

Many will be glad to know that at one New England Billiard Concern, a complete billiard-room outfit can be obtained.

This branch of the business is new, but during the present year an order can be left with us for a complete outfit. We measure the room, place the tables, fixtures, chairs, etc. in position. Making the combined price lower by saving separate profits. This we do on easy terms if desired, to enable those with small capital, wishing to commence business, an opportunity.

Articles Accompanying Tables.

Billiard table outfit consists of

One Cue Rack.	One set of Markers.
One dozen Cues.	Wire and Hook.
Four Ivory Billiard Balls.	Four Chalk Cups.
One dozen Chalks.	Two Bridges.
Four Bridge Hooks.	One set Rules of the Game.

Pool table outfit consists of

One Cue-Rack.	One Triangle.
One Ball-Rack.	One dozen Chalks.
Sixteen Composition Pool-Balls.	Six Chalk-Cups.
One Bottle.	Twelve Cues.
Sixteen Small Balls.	Two Bridges.
One set Rules.	Four Bridge-Hooks.

The ELECTRIC CUSHIONS are Up to Date.

Billiard Supplies.

Since our supplies have become so popular, many anxious to sell have untruthfully represented their goods as coming from Briggs.

To avoid deception, always look for our label.

Cloth just now is extremely difficult to choose, on account of the many inferior grades offered for sale. We are now using a cloth that has been selected after many years' trial, and can be recommended as superior for this purpose to any other in the market, being made of the finest well-dyed wool, hard-twisted, short-napped, and of extremely close web. In buying first quality see that "No. 1" in gold letters is marked next to the selvage edge.

SIZE TABLE	NO. 1 QUALITY	NO. 2 QUALITY
4½x9 for Bed and Cushion.	$20.00	$16.00
" Bed,	16.00	13.00
" Cushion	4.50	3.50
4 x 8 " Bed and Cushion	18.00	14.50
" Bed,	14.50	12.00
" Cushion,	4.25	3.25

Pockets are now made from leather as a novelty, although the old-fashioned worsted ones are still by far the most popular, having the advantage of adding a finish to the table.

Worsted Nettings per set	$2.00
Fringes	1.00
Leathers	.50
Nettings, Fringes and Leather	3.00
Leather Pockets	3.00

Ivory Balls are still used for billiards, although seldom for pool. Because of its scarcity, seasoned ivory can only be obtained from those carrying a large stock.

Write to us for latest quotations on well seasoned ivory.

Tip Glue has been another much needed article. A good glue has recently been made for this express purpose, put up in convenient cans and labeled with our label.

Glue—gill cans, with brush . . . . $ .25

(10)

The ELECTRIC CUSHIONS always make Friends.

Billiard-Room Clocks are made in either oak or cherry. The price has been reduced trusting that the many room-keepers now without any kind of price register may be induced to buy.

Time and Price Register, either in Oak or Cherry . . $15.00

Cue-Clamps are used for holding tips while the glue is drying, and are very useful in the billiard-room.

Cue Clamps . . . . $ .50

Cue-Cutters are now generally used, being far handier in tipping cues than the old "saw and miter box." A novelty is made from fancy wood, with nickel-plated handles and knife, which is very ornamental.

Cue-Cutters (nickel-plated, fancy wood) $2.00
Cue-Cutters (lacquered and plain wood) 1.00

Best Materials used in the ELECTRIC CUSHIONS.

Chalk is now mined in France, and put up there for billiard purposes. Money is saved by buying in original packages.

Chalk, (original package) per gross . . . . . $ .50

Composition Balls have largely taken the place of ivory for pool. This fact has led to placing many poor grades on the market, thus prejudicing many against all composition balls. The fact is that a very good pool ball can be made of composition if enough money is spent to do so. Our balls are made expressly for us and are warranted to the purchaser for five years.

Pool Sets (standard size) $25.00
Billiard Sets (standard size) 10.00
> Insist on BRIGGS' label.

Tips of good quality are difficult to find.

The French have for years past supplied the world with the best. In order that our customers may have the genuine article and to guard against worthless imitations every box is labeled, "Briggs' Own Importation."

French Tips (oval tops) $1.00
French Tips Prof. (square tops) 1.50

Cue-Cases are made from Leather or Canvas; their convenience merits their growing popularity.

Cue-Cases (Leather) $3.00
Cue-Cases (Canvas) 1.50

Cues were never made in so great variety of styles as now. The purchaser being able to select as fancy dictates, from 25 cents upwards.

For billiard-rooms those costing from $9.00 to $15.00 per dozen are in demand, while the individual usually indulges as his purse allows. Jointed cues are much used now on account of their convenience.

SPECIAL OFFER.

A jointed cue, hard wood butt, ivory tip with case, complete, $4.00.

THE ELECTRIC CUSHIONS will Outwear any Other.

PRICE LIST OF CUES.

No. 1. 3 joints, veneered, butt plate, name plate   ivory tip $5.00
No. 2. 3 ''   ''   ''   ''   3.00
No. 3. 3 ''   ''   ''   very fancy ''   15.00
No. 4. 2 ''   ''   ''   graved butt ''   4.00
No. 5. 2 ''   ''   ''   2.50
No. 6. 2 ''   ''   ''   '' very fancy ''   10.00
No. 7. 1 ''   ''   graved butt ''   3.00
No. 8. 1 ''   ''   ''   ''   ''   3.50
No. 9. 1 ''   ''   ''   2.50
No. 10. 1 ''   ''   ''   ''   3.00
No. 11. 1 '' butt, closely wound with cord   ''   3.00
No. 12. 1 ''   .   .   .   .   ''   1.50
Bamboo   .   .   .   without ivory tip $1.25   ''   1.75
Maple, beaded and turned   ''   ''   1.00   ''   1.50
Maple, fluted   .   .   .   ''   ''   1.25   ''   1.75
Maple, polished plain .   .   ''   ''   .50   ''   1.00
Ash .   .   .   .   .   ''   ''   .25   ''

IVORY JOINTED CUES

| No. 8 J. . . | $5.00 | No. 10 J. . . | $4.50 |
| No. 9 J. . . | 4.00 | No. 12 J. . . | 3.00 |

| Cues tipped, each . | .05 | Cues ivory tipped, 2 ends | 1.25 |
| Cues ivory tipped, each | .50 | Cues ivory jointed, each | 2.00 |

Novelties not quoted here always on hand. Any style desired made to order.

(13)

Home Tables with ELECTRIC CUSHIONS not Neglected

REPAIRS.

The first axiom of our business is good workmanship. When a new man enters our employ he is subjected to very careful training. His particular "bent" is discovered, and he is kept at that kind of work.

The men sent outside to repair tables are especially selected as to their adaptability, a record being kept of each man. This careful selection cannot be too highly over-estimated by billiard-table owners, as many good tables have been botched and ruined by men not thoroughly conversant with their trade. Our prices are as low as are consistent with first class work.

We consider it a favor if grievances will be reported at the office.

Price List of Supplies.

ALPHABETICALLY ARRANGED.

Altering Carom Table to Pool, including Pockets and Pocket Irons	$25.00
Balls—Billiard, Ivory. Latest quotation on application	
Balls—Billiard, Composition. Best, warranted five years	10.00
Balls—Pool, Ivory. Latest quotations on application	
Balls—Pool, Composition. Best, warranted five years	25.00
Balls—Small shake. Composition, 16 to set	.50
Bottles, leather	1.00
Bridges, each	.50
Bridge hooks, each	.10
Brushes	1.00 to 3.00
Bolts—cushion, per set	4.00
Bolts—cushion, re-plated, per set	1.50
Chalk, French, per gross	.50
Chalk, French, per dozen	.10
Chalk Cups, per set	1.00
Clamps, for tipping cues, each	.50
Clocks, time and price register	15.00

The ELECTRIC CUSHIONS will never make you Miss.

PRICE LIST OF SUPPLIES—CONTINUED.

Cloth . . . . see p 10.	
Covers, rubber . . . ., .	$3.00
Court Plaster, green, per box	.25
Cues . . . . see p. 12	
Cue Cutters	1.00
Cues tipped, each	.05
Cushions, *Electric*	50.00
Cushions, slow	35.00
Cushion Corners, false, set of 6	15.00
Cutting down Table to any size	40.00
Cutting down Table to any size and bevelling . .	60.00
Glue—tip, gill cans	.25
Legs, per set, ...	15.00
Maces, each	.75
Markers	2.00
Markers, Ratchet, Wire and Hook	3.00
Markers, to set on rail, French	8.00
Pins, per set	.75
Pocket Nettings, worsted, per set	2.00
Pocket Fringe, per set	1.00
Pocket Leathers, red, per set	.50
Pocket Nettings, Fringes and Leathers, per set . .	3.00
Pocket, made of leather, per set	3.00
Pocket Irons, per set	5.00
Pocket Irons re-covered, per set	3.00
Pocket Irons re-plated, per set	2.00
Polish, Scotch, per bottle	.25
Racks, cue	6.00
Racks, pool	6.00
Racks, private cue, one door	10.00
Racks, Private cue, 12 locks	18.00
Tips, Briggs' own importation	1.00
Tips, Briggs' own importation, Prof., (square sides.) .	1.50
Triangles . . . . .75 to	2.00
Turning and coloring Billiard Balls, per set . . .	1.00
Turning and coloring Pool Balls, per set . . .	4.00
Turning and coloring Pool Balls, ivory, per set . .	5.00

How to Set Up a Table.

A billiard table is carefully numbered. In setting up place portions similarly numbered together; No. 1 at the head, the others following from right to left. Tighten all bolts and level the frame.

After the frame is level place the slates in position (small holes on the edge answer for numbers) screw down perfectly level, cementing the screw holes and joints with plaster-of-Paris so as to make one solid, level surface. Then clean all particles of dust from the bed.

Stretch the cloth tightly over the bed and tack every inch. Put the rails on according to their numbers, being careful to tighten all bolts and level.

Nothing remains but to place the "spots" in position midway between the second diamonds from each end.

RULES FOR

BILLIARDS AND POOL.

Winning and Losing Carambole.

As formerly played at Roberts' Guildhall Coffee House, London. (Revised for use on the modern pool-table.)

The game as played in London had some technical points, which without revision would make it impractical for the modern American public. The revisor has tried to add only such points as would tend to popularize this old game and still keep its ancient value.

DEFINITIONS.

BREAKING—Placing the balls as at the opening of the game, and either giving a miss or striking the red ball as the player may choose.

BOCK—"String."

COUP—Pocketing one's own ball, either by a miss or by accident.

HOLED—Pocketed.

ODDS—The player receiving "odds" leads off.

RULES.

The GAME is PLAYED upon a six-pocket table with one red and two white balls. The red placed on the LOWER SPOT, situated 6 in. from the centre of the lower cushion. The game consists of "winning and losing HAZARDS, CAROMS and FORFEITS," and is usually played fifty up.

The LEAD and CHOICE of balls are determined as in the American game.

HOLING the white ball, (the winning hazard) counts two. Holing the player's ball from the white, (the losing hazard) counts two. Holing both on the same shot counts four. Holing the red ball, counts three. Holing the player's ball from the red, counts three. Holing both on the same shot counts six.

Each CAROM counts two. When two balls are struck, the player's ball, if holed, takes its value from the first ball struck. It will be seen that ten is the most that can be made at one shot.

(17)

Make a round table shot with the ELECTRIC CUSHION

The FIRST PLAY is from within the semi-circle, which in this game is of eight inch radius, described about the upper spot towards the head of the table with the string line as a diameter.

The RED BALL when HOLED or off the table is replaced on its own spot, or if that is occupied, on one midway between the two side pockets.

The OPPONENT'S BALL being HOLED or forced off the table is held in hand until the inning is finished, and then played from within the semi-circle.

The PLAYER'S BALL being HOLED is played from within the semi-circle.

A PLAYER CONTINUES to PLAY until failure to count.

If the player forces his BALL OFF the TABLE it counts one for the opposing side. If however he forces his own or adversary's off the table, after making a hazard or carom, he gains nothing by the stroke and his adversary plays without breaking the balls.

A COUP counts three for the opposing side.

A FAILURE TO STRIKE a BALL counts one for the opposing side.

The PLAYER'S BALL being IN HAND must pass outside the string before hitting a ball, failing he loses his turn and counts one for the opposing side.

If a shot is made with the WRONG BALL, and is discovered before the next shot, it is optional with the opponent to have the balls broken.

A BALL coming to a FULL STOP on the EDGE of a POCKET, and then falling in, shall be replaced and not counted.

If the striker's BALL be TOUCHED WITH the CUE prior to striking, it must be replaced in its former position.

THREE-BALL CAROM GAME.

The Three-ball Carom Game, is (as the name indicates) played with three balls, two white and one red. The billiard table has *three* spots in a line dividing the table lengthwise, running from the centre of the head cushion to the centre of the foot cushion. One of these spots, cutting the line in two equal parts, is called the centre spot, and the other two are situated half way between the centre spot and the head and foot cushions.

The spot at the head of the table is called the white spot, and the one at the foot of the table the red spot. The centre spot is only used when a ball forced off the table finds both red and white spots occupied. Therefore, should the white ball when forced off the table have its spot occupied, it would be placed on the red spot, or on the white spot if it be the red ball that is forced off the table.

In beginning the game, the red ball and one white are placed on the respective spots; the other white remains in hand, and is placed near the white spot previous to the opening stroke of the game.

(18)

The ELECTRIC CUSHION is always accurate

A player can take any position within six inches of the white spot, but he must strike the red ball first before a count can be effected.

In playing the game the following Rules should be observed:

The game is begun by STRINGING for lead, the player who brings his ball nearest the cushion at the head of the table winning the choice of balls, and the right to play first, provided the player's ball in stringing has not touched any other ball on the table. Should the player FAIL TO COUNT, his opponent makes the next play, aiming at will at either ball on the table.

A CAROM consists in hitting both object-balls with the cue-ball in a fair and unobjectionable way. Each will count one for the player. A penalty of one shall also be counted against the player for every miss occurring during the game.

A BALL FORCED OFF the table is put back on its proper spot. Should the player's ball jump off the table after counting, the count is good; the ball is spotted, and the player plays from the spot.

If, in playing a shot, the CUE is NOT WITHDRAWN from the cue-ball before the cue-ball comes in contact with the object-ball, the shot is foul. the player loses his count, and his hand is out.

If the balls are DISTURBED ACCIDENTALLY, through the medium of any agency other than the player himself, they must be replaced by the referee, and the player allowed to proceed.

If, in the act of playing, the PLAYER DISTURBS any BALL other than his own, he cannot make a counting stroke, but he may play for safety. Should he disturb a ball after having played successfully, he loses his count on that shot, his hand is out, and the ball so disturbed is by the referee placed back as nearly as possible in the position which it formerly occupied on the table, the other balls remaining where they stop.

Should a player TOUCH his own BALL with the cue, or otherwise, PREVIOUS TO PLAYING, it is foul, and counts one for his opponent, and the player cannot play for safety. It sometimes happens that the player, after having touched his ball, gives a second stroke; then the balls remain where they stop, or are by the referee replaced as nearly as possible in their former positions, at the option of the opponent.

When the CUE-BALL is very NEAR ANOTHER, the player shall not play without warning his adversary that they do not touch, and giving him sufficient time to satisfy himself on that point.

When the cue-ball is IN CONTACT with another the balls are spottde, and the player plays with his ball in hand.

Playing with the WRONG BALL is foul. However, should the player using the wrong ball play more than one shot with it, he shall be entitled to his score just the same as if he had played with his own ball. As soon as his hand is out, the white balls must change places, and the game proceed as usual.

(19)

No need of hitting hard with the **ELECTRIC CUSHIONS**

In match games the CROTCH is barred. The object-balls shall be considered crotched whenever the centres of both lie within a 4½ inch square at either corner of the table. When the object-balls are so within said square, three counts only will be allowed, except one of the object-balls, or both, be forced out of it. In case of failure by the player his hand is out, and the next player goes on to play with the balls in position as left by last player.

In this game no player is allowed to WITHDRAW before the game is out; by so doing he forfeits the game. The decision of the referee is final, but it might happen under extraordinary circumstances, that one of the players should believe his rights to have been violated by the referee; in such a case he must declare the subject of his grievance, and announce that he is playing the game out under protest. Then, should he lose the game, the subject of the grievance is left to the decision of experts mutually agreed upon.

OTHER FOUL STROKES ARE:

If, in the act of striking, he has not at least one FOOT *touching* the FLOOR.

If the player touches the cue-ball more than once in any way, or HINDERS or ACCELERATES it in any other way than by a legitimate stroke of the cue; or if, during a stroke or after it, he in any way touches, hinders, or accelerates an object-ball except by the one stroke of the cue-ball to which he is entitled.

As TOUCHING any BALL *in any way* is a stroke, a second touch is a foul.

Should a ball that has once come to a standstill MOVE WITHOUT APPARENT CAUSE, while the player is preparing to strike, it shall be replaced. Should it move before he can check his stroke, it, and all other balls set in motion by that stroke, shall be replaced, and the player shall repeat his shot, inasmuch as but for the moving of the ball, he might have counted where he missed, or missed where he counted.

It is a foul if the striker plays directly at any ball with which his own is in FIXED CONTACT, and the striker must in this instance play from balls spotted, as in the opening stroke of the game.

It is a foul to place MARKS of any kind UPON the CLOTH or cushions as a guide to play; also foul to PRACTICE the banking shot for the lead-off upon the plea of testing the balls, which until the moment of banking shall never be hit with a cue, and after banking shall not again be hit with a cue until the opening stroke is made; and it is also foul if the striker, in making a shot, is ASSISTED by any OTHER PERSON in any way, save by being handed the bridge, long cue, having the gas fixture moved and held aside, etc., by the marker or referee, after he has requested either to do so.

It is a foul against the non-striker, and the striker cannot make a count on the ensuing shot, if a ball in play is LIFTED FROM the TABLE, except it be unavoidable in those cases in which it is provided that, because of foul or irregular strokes, the balls shall be transposed or replaced.

(20)

In order to restrict deliberate PLAYING FOR SAFETY, it shall be optional with the non-striker, if his opponent makes a miss in each one of three successive innings, to accept the third miss or reject it and force his antagonist to hit at least one object-ball; and for this purpose that antagonist's ball shall be replaced by the referee. Should two balls be hit by this stroke, there shall be no count.

WHEN PLAYED AS A FOUR-HANDED MATCH.

In a four handed match—two playing in partnership against two—the foregoing rules of the single match must be substantially observed, with the following additions:

In this double match the player's partner is at liberty to warn him against playing with the wrong ball, but he must not give him any advice as to the most advantageous mode of play, etc., except it has been otherwise agreed before the opening of the game.

CUSHION CAROMS.

In this game CAROMS COUNT only when the player's ball goes to a cushion before hitting the second object ball.

If the players' ball is "FROZEN" to the cushion, in order to make the cushion a factor in the carom, the ball must be played against the cushion and made to rebound from it.

A DOUBTFUL cushion carom should be decided against the striker.

When the CUE-BALL is in CONTACT with either or both of the object-balls, it shall be optional with the player to spot the balls and play as at the opening of the game, or to play away from the ball or balls with which it is in contact, and count from a cushion.

The rules for three-ball game not conflicting with the above, also apply.

THREE CUSHION CAROM.

In this game it is necessary for the player's ball to hit three cushions at least, or a cushion three times to MAKE A CAROM.

A CUSHION cannot be counted as one of those necessary to a carom by playing against it, the striker's ball being FROZEN to it.

Rules of the cushion carom game not conflicting with the above, also apply.

BANK-SHOT GAME.

In playing the BANK-SHOT GAME it is necessary that the cue-ball hits the cushion before it hits an object-ball. This rule applies in LEADING OFF as well as later shots.

A CUSHION cannot be counted as one of those necessary to a carom by playing against it, the striker's ball being FROZEN to it.

The ELECTRIC CUSHIONS will outlast any other

The cue and OBJECT-BALLS being FROZEN, the striker must play with them as he finds them.

A DOUBTFUL bank-shot shall be decided against the striker.

The rules of the three-ball game not conflicting with the above, also apply.

KISS CAROM.

In playing this game the two white balls only are used. The game is played the same as the ordinary three-ball game, except the object-ball when spotted is put on the lower spot, and in order to make a carom the striker's ball must hit the object-ball, go to a cushion, and then hit the object-ball again.

BALK LINE GAME.

The bed of the table for this game should be divided into nine sections, by four lines drawn parallel to, and 8 or 14 inches from the cushions running clear across the table. The game is played like, and the regular rules for the three-ball game apply, except—

Should the striker's and an object-ball be FROZEN, he may if he prefers play in that position without spotting, provided he does not play directly against the frozen object-ball.

Should both object-balls be WITHIN one of the eight spaces made by the BALK LINES and the cushion, and then two caroms be made in succession without making either object-ball cross one of the lines, then the second carom does not count and the player's side is out.

A ball on the line is considered within it.

PYRAMID POOL.

The game of Pyramid Fifteen-Ball Pool is played with fifteen object-balls and one white ball. The latter is the cue-ball, and each player plays with it as he finds it upon the table, or from behind the string, if it be in hand. The fifteen balls are all of one color. Before commencing the game these fifteen balls are placed in the form of a triangle upon the table, a triangular frame being used for this purpose to insure correctness. The triangle is so placed that the apex rests upon the deep-red spot pointing toward the head of the table. Each player is to pocket as many balls as he can, and he who first scores eight balls wins the game.

THE FOLLOWING RULES GOVERN THE GAME.

In match or tournament contests the GAME is BEGUN by banking. The winner of the lead has the option of playing first himself from within the string at the head of the table, or obliging his opponent to play first from the same place.

Note.—When more than two play the order of play may be determined by lot.

(22)

Play cushion caroms with the ELECTRIC CUSHIONS

The player who makes the OPENING STROKE must strike the pyramid of object-balls with sufficient force to cause two or more object-balls to strike a cushion, or cause at least one object-ball to go into a pocket. Should the player fail to do either he must forfeit one ball to the table from his score, and the next player plays.

Should a player having NO BALLS to his CREDIT incur a forfeit, the first ball he scores thereafter shall be at once placed upon the table.

All strokes must be made with the point of the CUE; otherwise, they are foul.

When two players only are engaged in the game, he who pockets or scores eight balls first is WINNER of the game. But when more than two players are engaged, the game is ended only when the number of balls remaining on the table do not amount to enough to tie or beat the next lowest score.

AFTER the OPENING STROKE, each player must either pocket a ball or make at least one object-ball or the cue-ball, after contact with an object-ball, strike a cushion, under penalty of forfeiture of one ball.

A player shall FORFEIT ONE ball for making a miss, pocketing his own ball or forcing his own ball off the table.

If a player pockets one or more of the object-balls and his own ball goes INTO A POCKET or OFF THE TABLE he cannot score.

FORFEITED OBJECT-BALLS must be placed upon the deep-red spot, or, if that be occupied, as nearly below it as possible.

When the CUE-BALL is IN HAND, the player must play from within the string, and he is not entitled to play at any ball which is not outside the string. Should none of the balls be outside, that ball which is nearest outside the string must be spotted on the deep-red spot, and the player may play at it.

When the STRIKER is in HAND, should he play at any ball that is within the string line, or if, when in hand, he plays from any position not within the string line, without being checked previous to the stroke being made, any score he may make from such stroke he is entitled to; but if he is checked before making the stroke, and then makes it, it does not count for him; his hand is out and the next player plays, and all balls disturbed by the stroke must be replaced or left as they are, at the option of the next player.

Should the striker TOUCH the CUE-BALL in any way except with the point of his cue, the stroke is foul and he forfeits one ball. Should the player disturb an object-ball, the object-ball must be replaced by the marker in its original position, and the player loses his hand and forfeits one ball.

Should the player STRIKE the CUE-BALL TWICE it is foul; he forfeits one ball and loses his hand, and the balls (if any) disturbed in consequence of the second stroke are to be replaced in their former position.

Should a player PLAY OUT OF his TURN, it is foul, and the balls must be replaced in their former position, and he whose turn it is to play, plays.

But should a player PLAYING OUT OF his TURN make more than one stroke before being checked, the strokes so made are fair, and he is entitled to any balls he may have made, and to continue his play until his hand is out.

(23)

Depend on "English" with ELECTRIC CUSHIONS

Should any ball or BALLS on the table be DISTURBED by any other person or cause than the player, they must be replaced by the marker as nearly as possible in their former position, and the player must continue.

Previous to making a shot, the player must DISTINCTLY NAME the BALL which he intends to pocket, and designate the particular pocket into which he intends to put it. Should he by the same stroke POCKET other balls besides the ball he calls, he is entitled to all the balls he may so pocket. Should he fail to pocket the ball he calls, and by the same stroke pocket one or more of the other balls, the pocketed balls must be placed on the spot. Should he pocket a ball without naming or designating the pocket into which he intends to put it, the ball or balls which he may so pocket are to be spotted.

Should a player pocket a ball fairly, after having called the ball and designated the pocket, and afterwards TOUCH or DISTURB any OTHER BALL on the table, he is entitled to the pocketed ball; but he loses his hand.

PUSH SHOTS are allowed: that is, it is not necessary to withdraw the cue from the cue-ball before the latter touches an object-ball. When the cue-ball is in contact with another ball, the player may play directly on the ball with which it is in contact.

A stroke made when any of the BALLS are IN MOTION is foul. Should such a stroke be made, the balls are either to be replaced or left as they come to rest, at the option of the next player, and the next player plays. The striker loses his hand and forfeits one ball.

When two persons are playing, should a player incur THREE PENALTIES, scratches, or forfeitures, in succession, he shall forfeit every ball remaining on the table to his opponent Should more than two persons be playing then the offending player shall be adjudged loser of the game.

No player is allowed to WITHDRAW before the game is played out; by so doing, he forfeits the game.

41 (FIFTEEN BALL) POOL.

(By the courtesy of William P. Marshall, proprietor of the Marshall Billiard Parlors.)

Give to each player TWO SMALL BALLS, one of which is returned to determine the ORDER OF PLAYING. The other is retained to count from; no one else knowing its number.

Each player plays in turn, one shot to an INNING, counting all the balls he may get on that shot, the number on them being added to the number of his small ball.

When exactly 41 is made, the player or game-keeper DECLARES POOL, and the player the most distant from 41 is defeated.

POOL is also DECLARED when all the balls are pocketed from the table The nearest to 41 is the winner; the most distant is the loser.

A miss, or pocketing the white ball, is A SCRATCH, and the player so doing owes a ball to the table, besides what he may have scored on that

The ELECTRIC CUSHIONS are always the same

shot. If he has more than one ball in his rack, he can spot the one he prefers; if he has none, spot the first one holed. If he pockets more than one on his next shot, he can spot the one he chooses.

If a player gets MORE THAN 41, it is a burst, and all the balls he has scored must be spotted; the last holed, the nearest in the rear of the spot, and so on. In such cases he can have a new small ball if he chooses.

In PLAYING FOR SAFETY a player must cause the white ball to go to the cushion before or after hitting a ball; failing to do so is a scratch.

A player having NO BALL IN his RACK is worse off than one with a ball, regardless of its number or the number of the small ball he may have, and a player owing a ball is still worse off. A player making a BURST and NOT DECLARING it, must be credited with no ball.

All rules governing the Game of Billiards and not conflicting with the above apply to this game; push shots only excepted.

RULES FOR BOTTLE POOL.

The GAME shall be PLAYED on a pool table, with two plain red balls, a white ball called the cue-ball, and a leather bottle, such as is used for the game of pool.

The BOTTLE is placed in the centre of the table, standing on its mouth.

The TWO RED BALLS are placed on the regular spots on the table, as in billiards.

The ORDER OF PLAY shall be decided by lot.

The OPENING SHOT shall be played from within the string upon the red ball on the lower spot.

If the player FAILS to HIT the object-ball on the opening shot, the turn passes to the next, who shall play from where the ball comes to rest.

The game CONSISTS of thirty-one points, and is scored in the following manner:

A CAROM on the two red balls counts one.

POCKETING of a red ball counts one.

KNOCKING the BOTTLE down counts five, except in case explained below.

If the BOTTLE is KNOCKED DOWN by the cue-ball before hitting an object-ball, it loses five for the player.

TURNING the BOTTLE completely OVER on its base is game at any stage of the play, unless on the same stroke the white ball goes into the pocket or is knocked off the table, or a foul is committed.

KNOCKING the BOTTLE on to the floor counts game for the opponent at any stage of the play.

Mathematically correct angles with ELECTRIC CUSHIONS

There shall be NO SCORE placed against a player when he has no score.

POCKETING the WHITE BALL in any event, a miss or a foul, counts five off the score.

Should a player POCKET the WHITE BALL TWICE in succession, without touching either of the object-balls, he forfeits the game.

It is a foul whenever a player TOUCHES any BALL or the BOTTLE with the cue or any part of the person.

Any SCORE made ON a FOUL, or when the white ball is pocketed, shall not count in the player's favor.

When the BOTTLE is knocked down, it is to be SPOTTED, if possible, when it comes to rest on the table, otherwise it must be placed in the centre of the table.

When the BOTTLE, in any way, shape, or manner, RESTS upon a CUSHION, or is in or over a pocket, it counts five for the player, and shall be placed in the centre of the table.

Whenever it is necessary to place the BOTTLE on the CENTRE SPOT, and the centre spot is COVERED, the balls are placed as in the beginning of the game, the cue-ball being in hand.

A BOTTLE standing squarely on its mouth or on its base, and TOUCHING the CUSHION, is not to be considered as resting on the cushion.

When both OBJECT-BALLS are WITHIN the STRING, and the cue-ball is in hand, the play must be out of the string.

When either RED BALL is POCKETED or driven off the table, it shall be placed, if possible, on the lower spot; otherwise on the upper. Should it so happen that both spots are covered, the balls and bottle are placed as at the beginning of the game, the cue-ball being in hand.

The white ball KNOCKED OFF the TABLE counts the same as if pocketed.

A red ball KNOCKED OFF the TABLE is spotted, and if on the shot a count is made, the player continues.

It is the duty of every player to WATCH his own SCORE, and if at any time he exceeds thirty-one points, he shall start anew. His turn passes to the next player.

A FOUL to be VALID must be claimed by an opponent, and in case of disagreement it shall be subject to appeal. A MISS renders the stroke void.

PUSH SHOTS are allowed.

It is a foul if the player has not at least one FOOT ON the FLOOR in the act of striking.

TWO PENALTIES cannot be exacted for the same stroke.

When not conflicting with the above, the general rules for Pyramid Pool shall govern.

The ELECTRIC CUSHIONS have no Rival.

High Low Jack.

This GAME is PLAYED on a pool table, with a regulation set of pool balls. The fifteen ball is HIGH; the one ball LOW; the nine ball JACK; the highest aggregate GAME. High Low Jack and Game, each count one point to the possessor, the whole game being seven points.

The HIGH, LOW and JACK are of equal VALUE, the first holed taking precedence in making score.

In SETTING UP the TRIANGLE the three counting balls are placed in the centre, High in front.

When players have EACH ONE TO GO, a ball is often placed 2¼ inch from the bottom cushion and pocketed by banking it to decide game.

Rules for pyramid not conflicting, apply.

Continuous Pool.

This game is played with a regular set of pool balls. The game CONSISTS of a mutually agreed number of points, each ball pocketed counting one point. When all the BALLS are CLEARED from the TABLE, they are reset with the triangle, the player and play continuing without interruption until the number of points agreed upon be made by one side.

The CHOICE OF LEAD is determined by banking the same as in the American Carom game of billiards.

The opening stroke is played from within the string against the pyramid of object-balls and must drive two or more to a cushion or one into a pocket, failing to do either, two points are forfeited, the balls reset and the player tries again, and until a shot is made without forfeiture.

A player continues to play until he fails to count.

After the breaking shot the players must designate the ball to be pocketed or return pocketed ball to table and lose the inning. If more than one ball is named, to count, all named must be pocketed.

If a ball OTHER THAN the ONE NAMED be hit, the player need NOT pay the forfeit for a miss.

The OBJECT-BALL when RETURNED to the table must be placed on the lower spot or as near it as possible on a straight line below.

On each stroke the player must either pocket a ball or drive one object-ball or cue-ball, after contact with an object-ball, to a cushion under a penalty of forfeiture of one point. Should the CUE-BALL ALSO be POCKETED only one point is forfeited.

ALL STROKES must be made with the POINT of the CUE.

Each ball pocketed counts one for the player.

One point is forfeited for making a miss, or forcing the striking ball off the table. Should a ball be pocketed at the same time it is returned to the table.

Club Men Like the ELECTRIC CUSHIONS.

The cue BALL, being IN HAND, the play must be at a ball outside the string line from any point behind the string. Should there be no ball outside the string the ball nearest the string is placed on the lower spot. A ball on the line is within it.

The striker touching the CUE BALL in any way is counted a stroke, and subjects the offender to all penalties attached thereto.

The player TOUCHING an OBJECT BALL in any way, the disturbed ball shall be replaced or left and the player plays his shot or not as his adversary decides. In either case the turn is lost and no count can be made.

One point is forfeited if any BALLS are IN MOTION when a stroke is made. The turn is also lost.

The cue ball being STRUCK TWICE, the striker loses his turn and forfeits one point, the balls being replaced in their former position if desired by the opponent.

Two points are forfeited for playing OUT OF TURN if discovered before the second stroke is played. Should more than one stroke be made, the player plays his innings out, the opponent playing the next two innings in succession.

In case of outside DISTURBANCE OF BALLS, they are re-placed as near as possible to their former position.

PUSH SHOTS are allowed.

Should a player with a CUE BALL IN HAND play from a point outside the string without being checked, the shot is good. Being warned and persisting his turn is lost and the balls disturbed by the stroke are replaced.

One point is forfeited when THE PLAYER'S BOTH FEET are not on the floor when striking. Should a fair shot be completed, pocketing a ball, and then the player touch or move a ball on the table, his turn is lost, but the pocketed ball is counted. A player making three forfeits in succession forfeits all the balls on the table. Withdrawal forfeits the game. A forfeiture must be counted before the next shot, or not at all.

THE NEW FRENCH GAME.

AS PLAYED IN PARIS.

×D

O B

C   A

DIAGRAM OF THE FIRST SHOT.

A. Red ball in position.
B. White ball in position for first shot.
C. Inclosed space, left hand corner.
D. Marked spot.

The OBJECT of this game is to drive the red ball inside the quadrant C, made with a convenient radius, by the white ball played from within the string line down the table.

The RED BALL is placed in the upper right hand corner, touching the side and end cushions. The WHITE, anywhere inside the string line.

The GAME is WON by the player who drives the red ball inside the quadrant in the least number of shots.

The WHITE BALL is PLAYED down the table, and must, before striking the red, go first to the left hand cushion, then the lower cushion.

The white ball for EACH SHOT is taken in hand, and played as above described.

After an inning commences, the RED ball must not be touched, but allowed to ROLL FREELY, as driven by the white.

Should the player, AFTER TEN SHOTS, fail to "corner" the red ball, then the inning is at an end. The red ball is replaced, as at the beginning, its place being marked, and the next player plays. At the commencement of a player's SECOND INNING, the red ball is placed in its former position, as marked at the end of his former inning.

DON'T!

Don't fail to brush the cloth each time the table is used.

Don't brush the cloth against the nap, but brush FROM the head of the table.

Don't let the table remain uncovered when not in use.

Don't let the cushion screws become loose.

Don't lean the cues against the wall but always keep them in a perpendicular position, thus avoiding warping.

Don't let the leather project over the point of the cue, thus tearing the cloth. Use sand paper or a file.

Don't blame the table when your ivory balls roll untrue, but send them to a maker to be put in order. Ivory balls are always getting out of round, no matter how well seasoned they may be, because ivory shrinks only one way.

Don't let the woodwork on your tables get dirty; take good care of it, rubbing with a soft cloth or using polish recommended by a maker.

Don't put polish on your tables which you know nothing about, as in many cases nice work is defaced or ruined by such treatment.

Don't let your table get run down. Have your cloth taken off and bed dusted, also a general overhauling every little while, which a good workman can do in a short time and at a small cost.

Don't let inexperienced persons tamper with your table.

· · INDEX · ·

Ingram Content Group UK Ltd.
Milton Keynes UK
UKHW022330050623
422929UK00005B/215